AIR Business Book

Start a Business with the Definitive Guide on Rental Property Investing with Airbnb and Maximize Your Booking and Profits

Anthony Vi

©Copyright 2019 by Anthony Vi

All rights reserved.
This document is geared towards providing exact and reliable information with regards to the topic and issue covered. The publication is sold with the idea that the publisher is not required to render accounting, officially permitted, or otherwise, qualify ed services. If advice is necessary, legal or professional, a practiced individual in the profession should be ordered.

- From a Declaration of Principles which was accepted and approved equally by a Committee of the American Bar Association and a Committee of Publishers and Associations.

In no way is it legal to reproduce, duplicate, or transmit any part of this document in either electronic means or in printed format. Recording of this publication is strictly prohibited and any storage of this document is not allowed unless with written permission from the publisher. All rights reserved. The information provided herein is stated to be truthful and consistent, in that any liability, in terms of inattention or otherwise, by any usage or abuse of any policies, processes, or directions contained within is the solitary and utter responsibility of the recipient reader. Under no
circumstances will any legal responsibility or blame be

held against the publisher for any reparation, damages, or monetary loss due to the information herein, either directly or indirectly.

Respective authors own all copyrights not held by the publisher.

The information herein is offered for informational purposes solely, and is universal as so. The presentation of the information is without contract or any type of guarantee assurance.

The trademarks that are used are without any consent, and the publication of the trademark is without permission or backing by the trademark owner. All trademarks and brands within this book are for clarifying purposes only and are the owned by the owners themselves, not affiliated with this document

Codice ISBN: 9798611102138

Table of Contents

CHAPTER ONE

INTRODUCTION 7

WHAT IS AIRBNB: HOSTING BUSINESS? 11

NETWORK ECONOMY VS SHARING ECONOMY
.... 14

THE CASE OF AIRBNB 18

CHAPTER TWO

WHAT DO GUEST REALLY WANT? 20

WHAT TO LOOK OUT FOR 26

THE BASICS 28

HOW TO CATER FOR BUSINESS TRAVELERS .. 33

HOUSE RULES AND COMMUNICATION WITH
GUESTS 36

CHAPTER THREE

TIPS TO GET YOUR HOUSE READY: INTERIOR
DESIGN WITHOUT PROFESSIONAL HELP 43

GET YOUR PROPERTY READY 47

SHARED ROOM LISTING 53

PRIVATE ROOMS LISTING 54

ENTIRE HOUSE (MAIN HOME) LISTING 56

GUEST HOUSE LISTING 59

VACATION HOME LISTING 62

CHAPTER FOUR

TAKING GREAT PHOTOS OF YOUR HOUSE: HIGH-QUALITY PHOTOS WITH YOUR SMARTPHONE 65

OPTIMIZE YOUR PROFILE 66

TIPS FOR TAKING QUALITY PICS WITH YOUR PHONE 68

CHAPTER FIVE

ALL THE TIPS YOU NEED TO KNOW TO CREATE AN AMAZING LISTING IN AIRBNB: WRITE AN IRRESISTIBLE AIRBNB TITLE AND SUMMARY OF YOUR PROPERTY 72

NO BULLSHITTING WORDS / UNNECESSARY ADJECTIVES 75

SURPRISE AND SPAWN YOUR READER 76

MARKETING / INFORMATIVE ADS 77

CLEAR ADS TEXTS 79

WRITE EXPRESSIVELY AND CONCRETELY 81

SPECIAL FEATURES 83

CHAPTER SIX

WHAT IS THE BEST PRICING STRATEGY: MARKET RESEARCH AND HOW TO FIND BEST ROI AIRBNB PROPERTIES IN YOUR AREA 91

THE IMPORTANCE OF THE RIGHT PRICE: CLIMB THE RANKING AND SELL 92

HOW TO GET STARTED 93

THE IMPORTANCE OF MARKETING STRATEGIES FOR AIRBNB 96

HOW TO BE SUCCESSFUL WITH AIRBNB STARTING FROM THE HOST FIGURE 102

AIRBNB PLUS 104

CHAPTER SEVEN

HOW TO HANDLE YOUR GUESTS DURING
THEIR STAY AND AFTER THEY LEAVE........... 109

HOW CAN I WELCOME MY GUEST?................... 109

WHAT ARE THE SAFETY RULES? 111

CHAPTER EIGHT

HOW TO BECOME AIRBNB SUPERHOST......... 117

WHO IS A SUPERHOST?.. 118

How to become Superhost? Airbnb requirements and considerations 119

Advantages, Rewards, and Benefits: Because It Is Better To Be an Airbnb Superhost.. 124

HOW TO STAY SUPERHOST: PROVEN METHOD
.... 127

CHAPTER ONE

INTRODUCTION

The economy of the world is changing every single day. There was an era where all things real estate was a thing of necessity, and even though people are living in great harmony with one another, there is always the need for some privacy and a sense of security. Many felt safe, knowing that there is always a place they can call their home – their place of abode. The history behind most of the knowledge we know about sharing economy has come a long way since those times. Technology has impacted the way we live in a number of ways. We can't fathom its impact by merely acknowledging the fact that many of the digital systems we have these days are as a result of many years of experimenting and testing by men of these early days, who made it their lives' purpose.

As technology improves and it began to experience tremendous advancement, so does the economy of men over the years. In recent times, the enormous growth that has been experienced in the sharing economy alone is nothing short of exceptional. The many ways in which men have managed to figure out a working economy that relied on sharing the excess of what you have in order to get the best out of the resources that which each individual is blessed with. In medieval times, there was the idea of a trade by barter where men exchange goods among themselves. Those who have foods exchanged with others that have clothing, and it was done amicably and efficiently. This type of sharing economy makes sense; so far, the participating parties are able to agree to the terms of the transaction, and by so doing, they ensure that resources are effectively utilized, hospitality is rendered, the community residents are empowered, and economic opportunities are presented to them in diverse ways.

Networked hospitality establishments have arose in recent years that, although mainly due to economic benefits, the offer of tourist accommodation and the way in which visitors experience their stay at a travel destination have been characterized by pioneering and unconventional innovations. These innovations were made possible by creating systems of network with which users could share their under-utilized goods that are also available for economic transactions. Airbnb comes in as a perfect example of a profitable peer to peer network platform available to all and sundry for sharing a part of their resources. Airbnb and traditional hotels are in constant competition for price and initially, the low-class hotels such as two or three-star hotels are those on the receiving end of the economic implication of Airbnb, however, as its network reach and the listings on the website begin to grow, the hotels on the upper part of the supply chain started feeling the impact as well. What sets it apart and made it so appealing to travelers is the fact that it had an experimental value to it that delighted many travelers: the wonder of having a whole new experience, the contact with the locals, plus interacting with the community, and living in residential areas all contributed to the decisions of guest around the world. They are on the lookout for the perfect adventure and the opportunity to witness the aura and cultural heritage of their destination.

The digitization of the market and the bilateral business model made exponential and continuous growth possible. Not only is this growth threatening the market share of traditional methods of accommodation, but it also mounts pressure on the housing market as a whole by helping to escalate the tourists' visitation quota and boost the local economy of the community.

Three dudes decided to lease out extra rooms in their apartment for an extra source of income. It started as a way of helping people find alternative accommodation at some fee – a simple act of benevolence at a small price. The startup experienced many tests and struggles amid several launches, before what was now known as Airbnb came into existence. They started out with the name AirBedandBreakfast, and the whole idea behind it leveraged on the sharing economy. It began as a completely offline company that meets the needs of people and offers them a completely new exploration experience for a much lower price than what the traditional motels charge. It has now become a successful online business that takes advantage of the creativity of the sharing economy and the substantial influence that technology has had on our daily lives in recent times.

Over five and a half years, Airbnb has stretched out its operational presence by going fully online and establishing its dominant presence in over 35,000 cities in 191 countries of the world. The sharing economy might still be in its early days and is growing rapidly; it is worth noting that its growth as regarding Airbnb is unusual. However, it is proof of the viability and success of the sharing economy in the modern ecosystem, as it will become an even more profitable business model in years to come.

WHAT IS AIRBNB: HOSTING BUSINESS?

Airbnb was founded in 2008 and has its

headquarters in San Francisco, California; it is an open-source online community marketplace. And it has come a long way to reach this stage. A marketplace for people to list their property such as an extra room in a house (and in some cases a complete apartment) to guests and get paid in return. Guests can discover cool spots in new places and go on interesting experiences organized by locals. Airbnb connects travelers and explorers with diverse cool experiences alongside having a firsthand local experience of the cultural heritage of the location where they are. It might be a spare bedroom, an apartment, a villa, or a beautiful cynic private island. Airbnb gives both the host and the guest flexibility while meeting the needs of all stakeholders.

One key attribute that makes the idea behind Airbnb to work is trust. Even though the system has a lot of users both hosts and guests, it wouldn't have been a monumental success that it is today if the trust between users is not there. The whole system is equipped with many safety tools, verification process that builds trust and solid identification process that enable both host and guests to check out each other before they actually meet physically. All forms of fear that the guest might harbor are easily allayed by reviewing the profile of the host to determine if they are a great fit for them.

It all began with recent university graduates who turned their home into an *"Air Bed and Breakfast"* by offering to help people with a place to stay overnight on-air cushions during a San Francisco conference in 2007. After originally starting off as a totally offline business, it transformed into a commission-based web-platform for room sharers and travelers. A few years later, the company stepped up their game and started offering exclusive deals that are way beyond air mattresses and people's spare rooms: with exclusive offers such as luxury houses in Paris for thousands of dollars, lofts in Manhattan for above $1000 a night, or real estates in Barcelona for a bunch of people, Airbnb stood up and became both a competitor and a disruptor for the traditional hospitality industry.

However, it is worth noting that the idea of a system of networked hospitality business models includes several other companies modeled in almost the same way as Airbnb. Examples such as HouseTrip, HomeAway, and Wimdu are worth mentioning. Still, Airbnb continues to be the market leader and most recognized company when it comes to the peer-2-peer (P2P) accommodation business.

NETWORK ECONOMY VS SHARING ECONOMY

Companies such as Airbnb and Uber have placed themselves in a very pivotal position as they form a significant part of the collaborative or sharing economy. Their positioning finds support among people who are of the school of thought that "sharing" should be considered as a term mostly used to for showing the interactive relationship that existed among each consumer. Some others view the sharing economy as a way in which consumers give each other temporary access to goods and facilities that were underused ("inactive capacity"), in exchange for money. By carefully analyzing the key features of this type of business model, it is evident that three elements distinguish the sharing economy from other forms of economy:

1. The sharing economy is based on person to person, consumer-to-consumer interactions. It is not about property rental from a company to consumer(s). There might also be a case product service economy, where consumers gain access to a product while the service provider still has the full ownership right.

2. The sharing economy deals with interactive relationships between consumers who give temporary access to a product one another without transferring ownership of the product. Therefore, the sharing economy differs from the second-hand economy due to the fact that goods are not outrightly sold or given to consumers (as is the case with online platforms such as Amazon or eBay).

3. The sharing economy serves as a more efficient use of real assets as it does not involve the case of private individuals providing service to each other. After all, physical goods can be left unutilized, but the same cannot be said

about human beings.

Internet platforms that bring together shoppers to offer services to each other represent the on-demand sharing economy. Task Rabbit is a great example of such a platform that allows you to employ people to work in your home.

The term hyper-connected economy can also be used when referring to the "sharing economy." While market platforms connect supply and demand between producers and buyers, digital platforms connect customers with almost everything on the internet. The online platform represents a generic 'ecosystem' that can link potential customers (prospects) with individuals and multinationals; so far, they are able to satisfy the want of the customer. Anyone can become a supplier of diverse categories of products and services at the push of a button. This is the immense impact of innovation and changes that digitization and digital platforms have brought upon us. The notion of "sharing economy" must be, however, differentiated from the traditional meaning of "sharing." The initial motive for sharing does not involve the exchange of money, and sharing only takes place in the absence of market transactions. What companies like Airbnb, Uber, Postmates or Task Rabbit have as a common feature is that they provide a platform for coordinating the demand and supply of in-demand products and services that were not initially available on the market. While people can rent out their property to strangers on Airbnb, Uber allows people looking for a taxi to quickly find a ride through an unprofessional or semi-real taxi driver who has suddenly become an entrepreneur. Task Rabbit connects supply and demand of tasks, Instacart for groceries, Postmates comes in handy for speedy deliveries of goods. It usually proves helpful to use any of these services, but you should know that they do not truly associate with the traditional meaning of sharing – which is to lend or give out only as a show of empathy and hospitality. The above-listed companies only represent a digital expansion of the market economy.

AIRBNB – THE DISRUPTOR OF TRADITIONAL REAL ESTATE

Airbnb, which started in 2008 as a simple proposal that combined economic benefits for travelers and income for residents of tourist areas, is a standard case in point of the sharing economy. As stated by Molly Turner, Global Head in charge of Civic Partnerships at Airbnb: *"Our business model is based on people who can't afford their homes and need extra money, so they rent out their homes."* The success enjoyed by the company can also be illustrated by the secondary effects of that basic proposition:

- a fascinating traveling experience: *"Live like a local"*;
- an easy to access an online platform
- the establishment of a trusted marketplace, through physical interactions and engagement
- the peer-to-peer online community (P2P), and networking power that leads to an increasing up-scale advantages

So far, it's been all about the experience: staying with someone, enabling contact between visitors and residents and doing tourism "off the beaten track," which makes it tempting to share the concept with real "shared" activities, especially the Sofa of branding, compare. This has led to an incorrect classification or Airbnb, in which individuals exchange assets (tourist accommodation), and both pay to a company that has set up a support platform such as "sharing."

Airbnb's concepts and economic impact are fundamentally different from sharing an asset as a mock model:

1. It is possible to discuss whether the apartment is underutilized. In any case, we see a replacement use instead of an additional use when a resident leaves his home to rent it.

2. The demand for vacation accommodation is much more elastic than for a typical electric drill.

3. In contrast to unused energy exercises, the short-term rental of private houses was in direct competition with an existing market. The economic impact has made Airbnb a disadvantage for the traditional hotel industry.

CHAPTER TWO

WHAT DO GUEST REALLY WANT?

Airbnb is not your regular hotel or motel, and it sure should offer a whole different level of experience to the users that are hoping to have a good time while out on your rental. No one wants to move in with a host that does not respect privacy or being too nosy or a property lacking in basic amenities. Normally, rentals on Airbnb are always cheaper than the conventional hotels, but the main reason that travelers and adventurers alike are choosing them over the more formal and business-like hotels is because of the less formal family experience that they bring with them.

They want to experience their stay in your city, just like you would as a local. And to top it off, they want to feel right at home while doing so. The fact that they contact you in the first means they saw something on your listing that they didn't see from your competitor. This means there is something that you are doing right and others haven't figured that out yet.

In the meantime, before other hosts get the memo and catch up, you are racking in a good amount of money. Many of the hosts think having a good listing on Airbnb is just about taking nice pictures alone (yes, don't get me wrong, you need the pictures), but more effort goes into having a great listing on Airbnb. Your guest has millions of listings to go through, and you should be aware that the host that has attained the status of a superhost didn't just get there overnight. It takes serious commitment to the satisfaction of your guest, and thoughtful thinking to provide amenities that will make their stay convenient. Proper and effective communication with your guest in the case of any misinformation to clear the air and make sure everyone is on the same page. Most of the time, the best listing has got good pictures (not bad, but also not so special), but the main reason why they stood out is that they are offering something other than the flashy pics on the listing that guest is actually looking out for.

Now you may ask yourself, what are your guests looking out for on Airbnb listing? Many at times, it not that they are actually looking out for something extraordinary or flamboyant; it's just that a simple establishment of trust through your past client via review can go a long way to wager their buying commitment in your way. The best of guest aren't looking out there for a state of the art apartment at peanut price, no, they are well aware of the effort and investment put into these things, and the next best thing you can do after putting out your best foot in your listing is to come clean. Let them have every detail so that they will know what to expect.

Put yourself in the guest's shoes for a moment. You are on your laptop or phone, going through tons of listing and earnestly looking out for the perfect one for your little getaway with the family. Most guest fire up the filter search tool, to help them sort through the huge listings on the website, and for your good, you will want to come up in that filter search. The very first thing that you do as a guest is to set the location of your vacay, and put on the filter tricks here and there to narrow things down and make your search more refined. As a guest looking to make an easy booking, you will look out for listings with flexible date fixtures, one that satisfies your present need in terms of location, accessibility to basic amenities, parking space, and a whole lot of little details that other hosts are neglecting.

To make sure that a guest selects your property listing on Airbnb among millions of other properties available, you have to stand out and offer something different, thoughtful, captivating and at the same time essential to your guest's convenience. Come to think of it, all of the amenities like mattress, couch, heating system, Wi-Fi and comfort are already mainstream basic and a giving in many a motels and hotels. How do you offer something different to what those guys out there in the traditional accommodation business are offering? How do you beat them at their game? How to up the game and outsmart them in a way that's not only convincing and exciting for your guests, but also full of joy and fun moment? You have the freedom to do as you like. No ceiling or limit at all. No policy to distract you from your goal, no slowing down through a protocol of decision-makers. Just you and your genius mind mapping out the route to a wonderful and successful listing on Airbnb.

As you flip through the pages of this book, you will discover all the right tools to arm your arsenal and develop a thoughtful listing that will get guest flooding to your page in a matter of weeks. Many are of the idea that listing property on Airbnb and appearing on the search page for guests is difficult. But in the following pages, I will divulge very simple ideas that you can implement and begin to see instant results. Not every guest is carried away by the flashy pics on your listing page. You have to go the extra mile and take care of all the little details that will prove if your listing on Airbnb is going to be a success or not. The following methods and idea are proven methods and tricks that work like magic, and even though after your guest have selected your location, and they still turned on the filters to streamline their search on Airbnb, your listing will pop right open before their eye because of the thoughts and efforts you have put into creating such an amazing property listing.

Before we go into discuss the details of the ideas that will help your listing rank on Airbnb search, here are a few tips to take note while creating your listing. If you do this right, you will be surprised by the immense results that it will produce.

Let's dive right into it. Firstly, you have to know that some guests are looking for a listing that is fixed for a particular date, however, your listing will only show up on a search that includes that specific sate. It is advisable that you employ a more flexible approach to give yourself more leverage and exposure. Also, one of the most important settings that you can make to your listing is to define the home type for your rental clearly. Airbnb has subcategories for the listing you can have on their site. And this is as a result of the demands of guests over the years. Listings are subdivided into the following types of apartments:

- **Total house**: Guests have all the space in the house to themselves. This usually includes a bedroom, a bathroom, and a kitchen. If you are on the premises with them, it is only logical that you indicate and let the guest know via the listing description that you are on the property with them albeit on a different floor or in a different block, as the case may be.
- **Private room**: In this category, the guests usually have their own bedroom. But the other areas in the house can be shared. In this case, the house rules are very important and must be clearly stated to make sure everyone is on the same page.
- **Shared room**: Guests sleep in a room or a common room that they can share with other guests.

WHAT TO LOOK OUT FOR

It is important to choose the option that best describes your listing type so that guests in order to give your guest a hint of what they are renting and avoid unnecessary expectations. As a host, the responsibility of describing your property in a clear and concise manner solely rests on you. Your listing must be able to communicate all the right information to your guest by mere scanning through it –it shouldn't be scanty and full of fluffy words, but captivating and enticing ones in a concise and brief manner (attention span of the internet is short at it may already). An equally important aspect of your listing is the price of course; you want to look at what others are doing and be sure that you are not shortchanging yourself. By setting a range of prices for your listing, Airbnb will automatically allocate a per night fee for your property. Also, be sure always to let your guests indicate the type of trip they are embarking on. Are they the "For Families" kind of trip or the "For Business" type. It is important to get all these details right.

Furthermore, if you would like to offer the instant bookings feature on your listing, this is a good way to increase your earnings and boost your listings on search results. You have all the control. Why? Guest are always in search of convenience, and the idea of instantly booking a place on their trip sounds very inviting, and as a host, you are always getting reservations from a guest that are looking to book a place as fast as possible. To screen out potentially frustrating guest, you can request that other hosts recommend them or that they submit a government-issued ID. You really got a lot of options and with instant booking, you can cancel any instant booking that you are not comfortable with (the guest broke your house rules or you are simply not okay with the reservation) by applying the penalty-free cancellation. With penalty-free cancellation, you will not pay a fee, lose Superhost status or receive any of the cancellation penalties. However, it's advised that you do not abuse this feature, as Airbnb is watching closely and will ban your account if they sense any form of foul-play. Lastly, always lookout for the following little filer details that your guest is always keen about; a number of bedrooms, free cancellation, specific facilities, special feature homes like a treehouse, campers, or boats.

THE BASICS

Return to the basics and think about what the guest really needs. It is important to have a contact book with emergency numbers and the host number as the key to facilitate communication. WiFi is now a popular place for guests and they hope they can connect online. Clean bed linen and towels are a matter of course. Store toilet paper in the bathroom. Basic toiletries such as conditioner, shampoo, and body wash must also be provided. They don't have to be brand A; they just have to be available. If there is a kitchen, liquid hand washing (soap is not so hygienic or inexpensive), liquid detergent, detergents, tea towels, cutlery, and dishes are crucial for those who want to prepare homemade meals and keep the place sharp. Span later. It is up to the host to provide guests who arrive sooner or later with coffee, tea or simple snacks. However, this can be a thoughtful and generous addition.

Clear services

It's easy to ignore the things you live with every day, but guests want to know exactly what to expect. If a list says there are a washer and dryer, but does not mention that it is shared with 20 other apartments, a traveler may feel disappointed. If you have WiFi that works everywhere, except in the guest room, a simple "WiFi" in your entry is not enough. You may not allow pets instead, but it's important to explain that you have one yourself: not everyone is cat-friendly, and allergies to pets are serious issues. Entering details makes the difference for a guest and prevents potentially disappointing experiences.

Washing Machine

Traveling with clothes can be very difficult. When vacationers travel to beaches, forests or amusement parks, they can purchase places where they can enjoy their beautiful memories. Who wants to wear clothes for every day of a long vacation? Washing clothes while traveling is more convenient. For these reasons, many Airbnb users are looking for rental lists with access to a washing machine. To make your bathroom even more attractive, provide guests with detergent and fabric softener.

Well Equipped Kitchen

Especially during a long trip, eating for

breakfast, lunch, and dinner can be exhausting, expensive, and slow. Guests want to be able to cook themselves. One of the biggest advantages of living in a house rather than a hotel. Give your guests access to your kitchen and to pots, pans, cutlery, plates, and everything they need.

TV/Media

Traveling is both about relaxation and activities and relaxing in front of the TV is one of the most popular hobbies for Americans. Even if you only rent a room in your house, make sure that the room has a TV. It's even better if the TV has access to premium cable channels, Netflix, Amazon Prime Video, etc. Guests can feel even more comfortable with a DVD and/or Blu-ray player, especially if they have a collection of popular films to choose from.

Air Conditioning

Nobody wants to fight to sleep in stifling heat during the holidays. To have a successful Airbnb, it is very important to have sufficient air conditioning. Even if it's not common in your area, central air conditioning controlled by a thermostat is the best option to keep all guests happy. Make sure every room you rent has access to a thermostat so guests can control the temperature in their room.

WiFi

The world works with WiFi, and your Airbnb gets bad reviews if your guests can't keep in touch with loved ones, the latest news or (sigh) their jobs while staying in place. To make your customers feel more secure, you need to set up a guest-only Wi-Fi network and give it a professional and legitimate name. Change your WiFi password for each guest and assure your visitors that no one else has the password. According to a consumer survey commissioned by Airbnb, an overwhelming 97 percent of US travelers surveyed say that services affect their travel experience. And while accommodations have the greatest impact on vacation quality, service is second for US travelers. UU. For Brazil, India, Italy and Mexico, however, the rule initially applies.

HOW TO CATER FOR BUSINESS TRAVELERS

Business customers naturally have different requirements. An ironing board or number for the next laundry service is useful for organizing business attire. Wi-Fi is vital and also additional iPhone chargers. Information on transport services and taxi numbers or free parking spaces is also an advantage. However, there is a strict criterion for obtaining the "Ready for Business Travel" certification. The hosts must provide a full list of houses or apartments (and the correct type that can be checked on Airbnb). The offer must not have pets on the property and must be a non-smoking area. Business Travel Ready services must include a workstation suitable for a laptop, Wi-Fi, self-check-in (including the key box, keyboard, smart lock or luggage rack), a smoke detector and carbon monoxide, essential elements as in the basic area Irons, hangers and a hairdryer. Submissions must have at least three stars before they are eligible.

Little Bit of Experimentation

Every few months, you should spend a night or two at your rental properties. The only way to pick out ways in which you can improve your property is by spending some time in it. You get to have a firsthand experience of what it feels like to be pass a night there. You will be able to detect minor improvements that can mean a lot to your guests. It might be adding an extra blanket, unclogging a drain, or including a bedside charging station; there is always something small and inexpensive that you can improve that can make a big difference.

A Little Extra Toppings

When a guest arrives tired and exhausted at your property, it will be thoughtful to provide them with all the help they can get. It wouldn't hurt to leave something cool as a bottle of wine on the counter for your guests. Some might argue against it but by doing so, you are offering just a minute percent of the hundreds of dollars that they are paying you. If you want to give them a gift, you can make it a little bit personal for each guest, depending on the type of guest you are having.

Free Parking Space

Your guest will be hoping to find a free parking spot on your property. It's a really nice incentive to get bookings to your lodge. If there is an option of free parking, you should let your guest be aware of that. Another thing to consider is the type of parking facility that you have (if parking space is available). It can be covered or uncovered. If it's covered, what kind of vehicle can it accommodate?

Swimming Pool

Kids and even adults are fascinated by the idea of lodging in a home with a pool. One of the most searched features that guests look out for in any listing is a swimming pool. However, be sure to keep the safety of your guest in mind by keeping the pool clean and safe with an annual inspection. Also, when a pool comes with towels in an easy to use location, your guests will be happy for it.

Recreation Guests

If guests stay for pleasure, it's a fantastic plan to treat the list as a hotel and make extra efforts to create a "home away from home" and additional resources at the destination. Just like in hotels, these are the little details that make a stay special, which is why guests prefer to book an Airbnb. Luxury soft beds, toys for the little ones or a complete city guide with highlights are just a few examples. Since most families cook, a well-stocked kitchen is beneficial for them, while friends or couples prefer recommendations for local restaurants. Children love to play in the room or in fun objects.

HOUSE RULES AND COMMUNICATION WITH GUESTS

It is important always to let your guests know of the house rule that you operate to bring everyone on the same page. They, however, can verify this by themselves in the check-in process, house rules, and the "Interaction with Guests" section, or by opening the top listing part hitting the "read more about the space" section. Here they'll better understand if you live near or on the property if they can check in all by themself or via a lockbox. This way, they also get notified of any other specifics that's pertinent about the property.

Usually, as hosts, you are open to as little or as much communication as you'd like. One thing to keep at the back of your mind is to make sure and double-check by asking if they had reviewed the house rules. Your list might contain rules such as no smoking, no parties and night-out times, quiet hours, and pet policy. With this in place, the guest will have no choice but to come clean and let you know of any other plans that different for the house rules, and if they didn't, they violated the rule and are liable to face the consequence. Also, make sure to clearly state your conditions that you think are not up to standard under the "You Must Acknowledge" section. You may decide to list a security deposit charge here for damages. When the guest books your space, they're acknowledging and agreeing to these terms.

Be Friendly

Most guests respond to hosts that communicate in a friendly manner. And whenever their messages pop up on my phone, I reply to such notification swiftly. By trying your possible best to be as friendly as possible to your guest, you are giving yourself the opportunity to build some form of rapport. This will give you the leverage when it comes to securing a booking for them. Airbnb requires that both the host and the guest exchange couple of messages in a back and forth manner, and this can be require some patience. If you have connected with your guest in some level, they will be happy to stay and actually get a booking from you as opposed to jumping on the next best opportunity out there.

LEGAL SIDE OF THINGS

Airbnb's legal issues are regularly in the news due to zoning and administrative codes, but mostly you as the host are concerned about it more than the guests. Airbnb's help section states that "*Some cities require hosts to register, get a permit, or obtain a license before you list your property or accept guests. Certain types of short-term booking may be prohibited altogether.*"

It is the duty of the host to search by your locality on the Airbnb with the keyword: *"responsible hosting in my location"*. This way, you'll be able to know the right steps to take in setting up a listing that is both legal and stress-free. Certain Airbnb projects, especially in urban areas like New York City, where this is a known issue, will state if your listing can be considered a legal listing or not. When it is perfectly done, the occupancy tax available to you as host in certain jurisdiction serves as a watermark to a guest to show that it is definitely a legal listing.

Protecting yourself

To give yourself some form of protection against the negligent guest, and to safeguard your property, you can ask for three-stage online verifications to screen out such guests.

The fact that they do not respect the space might put too many of your amenities in the way of damage. The type of details that you can ask from your guests include driver's license details; this enables you to be able to contact guests directly after that in case there is the need for it.

Cancellation Policy

As a host, you can set your own cancellation policy from three available Airbnb-standardized policies: Flexible, Moderate, and Strict. You'll need to clearly state the cancellation policy in the listing, so that your guests can note the terms before they book your place, and know what, if any, part of the price is refundable for changes or cancellations. In some cases, you may decide to grant your guest a refund irrespective of the cancellation policy depending on whether they reached out to you.

LOCATION OPTIONS

Maintaining your privacy as a host is important, but no matter how you value your privacy, your guest still needs an estimated location of where your rental. This is an important part of their decision-making process. How accessible is the place to nightlife, markets, and restaurants? For the busy type of guest, Airbnb has a feature known as the Airbnb Plus. In this case, Airbnb does the work for the guest, as it checks out those listings for exceptional quality, consistency, design, and comfort. Note that all Airbnb Plus homes are visited in person by company personnel. So, if you plan on listing your property as an Airbnb Plus property, be ready for their visit. They usually check for a whole list of things that guests told them that they love, ranging from must-have amenities to the art on the walls."

A guest can easily find your property once they've filtered their search accordingly with search filters corresponding to your listing features. They can search for a specific area on a map for listings with the above knowledge. It is a great feature for those who know exactly where they'd like to be in a city. We said that guests wouldn't find out the exact address until they've confirmed booking for the majority of listings for safety and privacy concerns; however, Airbnb will still provide some additional information.

CHAPTER THREE

TIPS TO GET YOUR HOUSE READY: INTERIOR DESIGN WITHOUT PROFESSIONAL HELP

If you are planning on renting out your house, then there are a lot of things that you have to take into account. It must, of course, be clean and the potential tenants must immediately feel at home upon arrival. I will walk you through all the steps you will need to take to get your house ready for Airbnb listing. With the following tips, you will have a new tenant in no time! Airbnb listings are increasingly seen as a fully-fledged alternative to a hotel room. Renting out a room to tourists yourself through Airbnb can be hugely profitable, but you have to pay attention and get a lot of things right. Your home must, of course, be equipped for everything that your guest throws at it. Follow through the pages below and discover amazing tips that blow your guests away. Furnishing your home for rental through Airbnb requires the right approach to getting it done correctly!

Before diving into the small print of various interior designs that are peculiar to different listing types (shared room, private room, whole house, vacation house), I'll like to address the general tips to getting your property started as a successful Airbnb listing.

Let the whole house be equipped and ready with all conveniences working perfectly. Tenants can be persuaded faster if there is already a floor, a kitchen with appliances, and maybe even neutral curtains. Simply because the tenant himself does not have to do much about the house and can enter it in no time. It is just an investment, but especially when you are planning to rent out the house for a longer period, it is definitely worth it!

Another thing to put in mind is to focus on the benefits of the house. Does the house have a nice view? Curtains open! Does the apartment have a nice balcony? Leave the path to the doors open so that potential tenants can easily find their way to the balcony. And remember, a lick of paint works wonders all the time. You should give dark walls a white lick of paint. We like a colored wall, but dark red or matte black does not suit everyone. White or off-white always work well. A house with light walls always seems larger, and that is exactly what you want!

Furthermore, be sure to store away important items like jewelry, personal documents, fragile items, and other invaluable things. Even though things go according to plan most times, you cannot always be sure that your guest is going to behave properly during their stay. So, it is always best to be safe than sorry. You cannot always be on-site to monitor things, and Airbnb is against the idea of spying on your guest with a hidden camera. The best bet is to maintain total discreet and keep your precious items away and safe.

You can also make available good storage space for keeping random kinds of stuff like wallets, keys, phones, journals, and so on. This will come in handy for your guest. By keeping a storage space, you are ensuring that your place is clean and ready for use. Nobody wants to be in the other's mess. And for tired travelers, nothing is as nice as 'coming home' in a beautiful house or apartment where you can throw your legs up. But also think of other things such as: remove the batteries from the smoke detector before it goes off as a silly thing or make sure that the first-aid kit is easy to find.

Finally, be creative with the whole idea and show your tenant what they can do with the extra space in the room. Many people like to see the space without furniture in it, but there are also plenty of people who cannot estimate the surface properly. Does the house have an extra small (bed) room, where you are afraid that potential tenants will break this off? Then place a bed and a closet in the room, so that the tenants can see that the extra room can also be used as a bedroom. The same applies to the living room. With a sofa and a dining table, you can see at a glance what is possible in the room!

Is My Home Suitable As an Airbnb?

The most important question is whether your home is suitable for including Airbnb. If you want to rent from a room, it must be large enough, easily accessible, and preferably the bathroom. Also, ensure that your guests have sufficient privacy.

If your apartment is not sufficient for Airbnb rental, a small renovation is always handy. It is important that you assess the costs in relation to the benefits. How to make ESA again to receive guests at home? First, it is important that everything works internally. Do you suffer from a dripping tap, an incorrectly emptied toilet, or a loose outlet? Then make sure you correct the shortcomings before your guests arrive. It is also important to order your house. Not only clean everything, pay attention to the kitchen, bathroom, and toilet, but also cleanliness. You place things that your guests can use, such as the remote control of their TV, in a logical place that is easily accessible.

GET YOUR PROPERTY READY

Advertise your place on Airbnb and earn some extra money through free to rent rooms or simply switch your entire house or an apartment, as a good idea (in fact, is a great and brilliant idea), but you are willing to get into the Work at least that's standard. More than 200 million people are using Airbnb since they started operation in 2008. In January 2018, according to the online hosting site, Airbnb had more than three million entries in 6,000 cities and 191 countries.

And here is a random but interesting fact: more than 1,400 of these entries were in castles. Yurts, buses, gypsy cars, windmills, and treehouses can also be rented. You can probably add any type of accommodation that you have on Airbnb. It's a great way to earn extra money, but it is work, and there is much to do before your first guest arrives. Here are some ways to eliminate - disorder and your place to organize, so the willing customers, and ensure that your Airbnb experience from the start is positive.

Renting your property at Airbnb can be a huge extra hassle to increase your bank balance so that you can enjoy some extra benefits. In 2018, the hosts won an average of £3,100 a year for their homes to rent around 36 nights a year. But even if your pride, one to his host's first-class, it is not the same as you, your room, or your whole house to leave strangers if you have friends who stay over the weekend. Fortunately, only a few simple adjustments are needed for each room to keep you and your guests happy. Then you can sit back and wait until the five-star rating arrives.

The Bedroom

This is the room where guests probably the majority of them spend time creating a cozy atmosphere is created. It is very important to see your home through the eyes of potential guests. Simple handles such as extra pillows, flowers, nozzles, and lamps are easy to use, but convey the feeling of luxury. Needless to say, but especially that the room is spotlessly clean. The next most important thing is, of course, the bed. If you want to earn real money from home, making sure to buy a new mattress (or at least cover a visco-elastic foam) may not be a bad idea. If you live in new parts as they invest, although their initial costs increase, you can recover the money quickly and generally require more.

Whether you keep your original mattress or not, make the bed with quality linens made of solid material (no polyester!) For the room more comfortable to make. You can opt for the white - look classic, but in some cases, add a touch of color depending on the season or type of guests you expect refreshing and can be effective. It can also be as simple as adding a set of light pillows.

I recommend a glass bottle with water to keep the barrel and glasses on the bedside table, along with some flowers in the room feel freshen up. You don't have to spend the country; only a few daisies and the like can be a subtle salute his. Make sure there are many hangers in the cupboard and that there is an extension cord so that your new friends can charge your electrical devices at night.

The Bathroom

A bath should be a refuge and a place to relax, and this is a sure way to earn extra brownie points. Once you've cleaned the place, you can step into some square one in the back push to borrow. Create a more luxurious shower experience by buying high-quality hand soap and shower gel that smell wonderful and invest in a few soft towels. Colorful towels for guests can be a good way to add a little fun to the interior of your bathroom. Some coffee table books and magazines also add interested in this space.

A scented tube diffuser creates a pleasant scent in the room and you don't have to worry about guests leaving candles burning accidentally, which can be dangerous. You need a simple toilet set save for the case that forgets and a hairdryer. Finally, place two containers in the bath, one for the waste and the other for recycling, in order to prevent the reel holders , and empty plastic bottles come into the container.

Kitchen

One of the benefits of renting an Airbnb is that when you cook at home, you can save money on expensive meals that you don't get when staying in a hotel. However, guests do not know your kitchen as

well as you. Protect your work surfaces and kitchen utensils against travelers with culinary problems. When a saucepans special guest buys, be your spell damage and if you have the placemats at hand, protect your work surface from burns. Make sure you have basic provisions in stock such as cutlery and kitchen utensils, cleaning fluid, towels , and kitchen rolls. Sometimes you will be surprised by requests for things such as eggs and kitchen utensils for your guests' children. A set of matching gloves and tea towels help the room to join. Again, it is very important to thoroughly clean the room. In this regard, clearly mark your baskets of cardboard, plastic, glass, and food waste paper to ensure that everything is disposed of correctly.

The Living Areas

Travelers are thanked for a lounge where they can enjoy their downtime. But keep it neat; because the disorder is one of the most important ideas that discourage people. Where possible, hide items from dressers and coffee tables to keep the center of gravity of the room simple and clean. Plants and flowers can bring a room to life if you have ordered more personal items. At the entrance to provide a doormat and shoe to ensure that guests can clean their shoes and storage without the mud at home to steps. A coat hook is also a reflective touch. It's a very good idea to keep valuables in a safe at home, just for your own reassurance.

SHARED ROOM LISTING

A shared room offers a no private place to sleep, which means that all share the space with the host, other guests, or both. Youth hostels fall into this category, but even if you provide the sofa bed in the living room to a guest, you can see a list of shared rooms.

How your room to prepare the list of shared rooms on Airbnb

- **Buy a folding bed or bunk**: invest in a good sofa bed or bunk beds for multiple guests without much space to take.
- **Create privacy**: Panel dividers or curtains divisions in the area offer sleeping area can hang a little more privacy for the shared rooms and are easy to store or bind when not in use is.
- **Blackout Sleeping Area**: When you rent your living room, you need to

invest a few curtains to make your guest's privacy and protection from the bright morning light on offer.

- **Provide a station for guests**: Install a rack - guest or organizer cubes with toiletries, towels, blankets, and other essential items so that guests can find them easily.
- **Choose hidden storage**: Ottomans and coffee tables with integrated storage offer your guests a place where they can store their belongings.

The most important advice for renting a shared room is that you know exactly what you are offering.

PRIVATE ROOMS LISTING

This list is closer to the bed and breakfast model on which Airbnb was established. In private rooms, guests can have their own sleeping area, with some shared areas such as the bathroom and kitchen. Renting a room through Airbnb is more than just offering a sofa bed for surfers. Your guests expect the service they are in a hotel used to be. Make therefore sure that the sheets freshly washed and ironed is present, as well as extra pillows and blankets, coffee and tea, and a copy of the rules of the house. Make sure your guests enjoy your Airbnb. In this way, make you sure, that in the future well done checks and other reservations.

Prepare your room for private room listing on Airbnb

- **Safe sleeping places**: with digital locks on the bedroom doors, guests can feel safe during their stay.
- **Optimize memory Guests**: take the maximum space available through the use of places such as hooks on the back of the doors and shelves hanging in the closet.
- **Allow accessibility in the kitchen:** People who rent private rooms may want to keep costs down, cooking holiday at home. Offer your guests a room and resources to make some meals at

home. Even though it is just a microwave and a kettle.
- **Invest only in guest resources**: if you have any kitchen utensils or groceries that you want, you may need to invest in individual guest appliances.
- **Managing the expectations of guests**: Make a list of everything you can and describe in detail of what stay in your house would look like. Always take into account the expectations of the guests, it is important.

ENTIRE HOUSE (MAIN HOME) LISTING

The idea for your whole apartment or house to a complete stranger to rent, while others enjoy it makes some people afraid. In any case, for you may seem to achieve this too, you must have all the important details prepared and resolved. If you do this correctly, it can make a difference whether you achieve this Superhost status or not.

Prepare your Main Home for Airbnb Listing

- **Provide a cupboard for the owner**: save your belongings with a closed cupboard for the owner.
- **Opt for obstacle-free zones**: You can have an entire floor of the house rent and the basement as storage space for your gear to keep out of bounds, while guests get.
- **Lock cabinets use special**: Block every cabinet that it is not the case, people want to reach and store valuables in them.
- **Provide a workstation**: It is very important to give your business guests a place to set up their laptops and chargers. A small desk with a lamp, writing utensils, and power strip offers your work travelers a place where they can work productively.
- **Simple and safe Check-In and Check-outs**: A lock entry with a combo, the extremely useful when you are not to let anyone or anyone after your stay. A code is a message that was sent to them, and they can, if necessary, come and go for it.

- **Ensure Airbnb cleaning checklist**: it is easy to ignore in your own home messy places. Make a list of areas to be cleaned if you miss a place.
- **Take the time to clean:** wait one day between the losses if you are self-cleaning run. This way you have everything ready for the next guest. M due to the courtyard, laundry, and general thor ough cleaning takes some time and some guests arrive early.
- **Upgrade essentials**: the essential elements of the bedroom and kitchen for guests: necessities such as mattresses, bedding, towels, plates and glasses for new houses during the guests' stay can really be very useful.
- **Invest in cleaning equipment**: It is very important to invest in cleaning equipment, and one of the most useful tools you invest on is the carpet cleaner. You will find that it is a true lifesaver in the event of accidents, dirt, and stains. A good machine for cleaning furniture and carpets can save you hundreds of

dollars in cleaning costs.
- **Present your animals**: after the main tour of the house, give your guests a tour of the rest of the property with the animals. Something like a short briefing about that in the absence is not in the grass coming.

Thanks to Airbnb's collaboration with RemoteLock, hosts can easily update their room security and guest access. RemoteLock is integrated with Airbnb's backup software. This means that new and unique codes can be sent directly to guests for each stay, so there is no risk of losing keys.

GUEST HOUSE LISTING

If you have a boarding house or suite for parents-in-law, like most Superhosts at Airbnb, it is important to create an individual and separate room for your guests. Your guests can enter the suite through a door that separates the access path from the garden and the main entrance, while you can take another path that leads to the side

of the house and the stairs that go down. Then you can give guests clear instructions about where they should start and where your
space private must end.

Prepare your room on for Guest House Airbnb Listing

- **Give your own entrance**: make sure your guests can enter the room without passing yours. Install a solid or compact exterior door with digital locks to reassure you.
- **Create an illuminated walkway**: some weary travelers can arrive late at night. Make sure they go to bed with them to provide a lighted walkway that leads them to their guest.
- **Separate rooms if your guest suite is connected to your home:** Make sure your guests are safe and regardless of their living space feel. For added security, you can attach a chain security gate to the inner glass door leading to the rest of the house and the windows in privacy in addition to the guest places. To provide your guests a

sense of security, you can install the lock door securely on the inside door of the bedroom.

- **Provide cleaning products for guests**: Accidents happen, ensure that your guests can be cleaned and repaired without any problems, Emergency kits and supplies should be present, for their customers when they need to have.

- **Offers that accept pets**: If your entry Pets supported, the feeling of the partner of your guests welcome. If you allow dog treats, dishes of food and water, and toys: you must inquire how to clean up guests after their dogs. The large garden must be fenced to ensure that pet owners cannot let their dogs escape into the garden."

- **Keep exterior to the visitor-ready:** Secluded with clear full barbecue and your seat guests can use during their stay. The area must always be kept clean and tidy. Since there is extra work or expense to make this feature available to your guests really like, especially on the days and nights, during which the light is always a bit cool.

VACATION HOME LISTING

If you have a larger home like that of Jeremy and Melissa with four bedrooms and an area of 3,500 square meters in Colorado Springs rent, you need to prepare for large groups of eleven or more people for each job received. You can probably only get a higher price for space. But for this reason, your holiday guests will have high standards for the comfort of the house. Below are some tips for preparing your Airbnb home that can really "surprise" your vacation home guests with:

Preparing the room for the list of Vacation Homes on Airbnb

- **Update your fridge**: family vacation means family dinner. Make room for large groups to their food during the week to save by about to switch to a larger refrigerator.

- **Buy an ice machine**: vacationers consume a lot of ice between frozen drinks and refrigerators. Invest in a freezer under the counter to the ideal of your home to feast holiday make.
- **Update your AC system**: the very last thing you want to know about your guests is that the AC device is broken. Be sure to invest in regular maintenance of HVAC, cool head to keep and happy guests during their entire stay. If your AC system is older, you must fully update it.
- **Keep a list of helpers ready**: For the maintenance that you need a list of contractors to make so that your house runs smoothly. This list includes cleaning the house, plumber, electrician, and a maintenance staff for different jobs. You can quickly almost all find for deals on PostalMates .
- **Create a work grill station**: nothing says more about summer holidays than hot dogs on the

grill. Make sure your grill is perfectly clean and functional and provide grill accessories for your guests. In furniture and a perfect for little of the outdoor home at the local holiday expenses.

- **Offer activities for children**: some facilities for children make your house a place for the whole family. These facilities keep the children busy. Amenities such as hula hoop, basketball, football, large rubber balls, pit corn, badminton, bubble machines, etc. They are perfect for kids on vacation.

If you are familiar with renting your new holiday home, you may want to expand your business. If you intend you to manage multiple stores, you'll need to find a way to a daily track of things. This includes reservation plans, cleaning, maintenance, and repair programs.

CHAPTER FOUR

TAKING GREAT PHOTOS OF YOUR HOUSE: HIGH-QUALITY PHOTOS WITH YOUR SMARTPHONE

The quality of the photos on Airbnb is a decisive point in the success of your rental. That, does not, however, mean you have to spend way over your head hiring a professional photographer before you can get good, quality pictures for your listings. Not that photo should be considered as your primary medium for your reservations on Airbnb. The feeling they have to give is confidence: trust in yourself as a host and confidence in the cleanliness and quality of the accommodation where your visitors will stay.

Our advice is to take high definition photos at least of all the rooms in your Airbnb accommodation. It is good practice to take pictures of the bedroom, bathroom, kitchen, living room from two angles to give a better understanding of the arrangement of the rooms. Also take the equipment that you think is worth the cost of being mentioned (washing machine, as some travelers, don't take the time to read the descriptions - which is by no means a contraction to what the attention you need bring to the writing of the descriptions as we saw previously; in both cases, the efforts that you provide related to the same point: confidence. Then remember to take photos for AirBnB during the day in order to have optimal light and bring out the details

When photographing your home for your listing, I recommend the addition of some long colorful stems in vases and jugs on tables, on kitchen countertops, and on coffee tables. This will suggest to guests you care about the details. You can go with a scene-setting items like some loaves of bread, cup of coffee, bowl of fruits in the kitchen. This will make your picture detail-oriented, will portray you as someone who knows what they are doing.

OPTIMIZE YOUR PROFILE

Often overlooked in an ad, the optimization of your Airbnb host profile is essential. A complete profile allows you to build trust with your travelers before you even talk to them.

Just as we will see below for the photos of your accommodation, beyond the words, the presentation of yourself will go for a good part through the profile photo that you will choose. Opt for a photo where you are relaxed without being neglected and serious without being professional.

Photos for AirBnB

High-resolution photos are always the best choice, especially to attract the attention of customers, or, in the case of Airbnb, of those looking for an apartment or room for rent. To take beautiful and captivating photos, in order to attract the attention of users, just follow simple precautions. First of all, we advise you to upload images of at least 1024X683 pixels. If you do not have a quality or professional cameras, photos taken with a mobile phone are also fine, the important thing is to respect these dimensions. Another not less important trick is to post photos horizontally.

Mistakes are a great opportunity to improve your results with very little effort.

- **Low Quality**: Grainy, dark, burnt photos, little pitch won't help your listing ad. This can only be resolved with a serious camera and the ability to use it.
- **Too Many Details**: The photos must give me the information first and the atmosphere after. Not ten pictures saying the same thing.
- **Too many or Too Few**: How many photos should be taken? It depends on the size of the accommodation.
- **Low Illumination**: Take your pictures in a bright and lively setting, like in the morning when the sun is well up.

Not that these are the only mistakes made by hosts when taking pictures for their list, however, the above mistakes are not uncommon.

TIPS FOR TAKING QUALITY PICS WITH YOUR PHONE

The photos with the smartphone are now increasingly fashionable; there are also commonly used for professional purposes. Let's start by saying that in the latest generation of smartphones, the cameras are on average good. Of course, often and willingly, some need an expert photographer to make the best of it. Fortunately, however, many of the adjustments and tricks that can improve the quality of taking a photo are easily applicable to everyone. Even by users who are less familiar with photography and technology. Before taking good pictures, you will need a little practice. Here are tips to improve your mobile photography for your Airbnb listing ad:

- **Clean the camera:** A very common mistake is that of not cleaning the camera, especially the back of the phone. We consider that most of us, at home, on the road or in the office, keep the phone with the rear camera resting on desks and furniture that are often not very clean, without considering the lint that can stop on the lens when we insert the phone in pants or backpack. A dirty or slightly greasy lens will present darker photos with slight blurring. It is highly recommended to clean the camera often with a microfiber cloth.

- **HDR mode:** To restore light and quality to your photos, you may want to start shooting in HDR mode. This technique is not recommended in all light conditions, but in low light or dark places, it can make a big difference. Some camera phones have this mode by default, while others just don't have it, especially in older models. Don't worry though, on the Play Store and App Store there are several applications to simulate the HDR effect on your smartphone.
- **Beware of filters:** With the advent of Instagram, filters have been the salvation for many. In addition to the famous social network, several applications work on the camera to apply filters when shooting. And many phones have filters set by the manufacturers. These filters, if we have no knowledge of photography, can even worsen our shot and above all, make it fake. The advice is to use the app only post-production and not those that work directly on the first shot. A good example can be PicsArt.

- **The Rule of Thirds:** This rule is, in fact, a rule of thumb that should always be followed before taking a photo. This rule is basically to divide the screen into nine grids, all the same. At this point, the object or subject must be positioned at the point of intersection between two lines of the grid. In the end, it is a very easy rule to apply, but which will change the quality and dynamism of your photographs.
- **Be wary of the Flash:** If there is little light, you use the flash. You are mistaken. Many of us tend to mislead the flash based on the poor lighting conditions of the scene to be captured. Be careful though, because the flash, in most cases will ruin the quality of your photos. It must be said that the technology in this field has evolved a lot, and now there is a double LED flash on smartphones, but still, it is not enough to recommend regardless of the use without considering the unpleasant red-eye effect on the subjects.

CHAPTER FIVE

TIPS YOU NEED TO KNOW TO CREATE AN AMAZING LISTING IN AIRBNB: WRITE AN IRRESISTIBLE AIRBNB TITLE AND SUMMARY OF YOUR PROPERTY

The title of your Airbnb ad, along with your main photo, determines whether or not they click on your ad. So take your time to craft a good title! Be specific and focus on the unique plus points of your home and state what the guest wants to read. You have 50 characters, use them well! Your advertisement on Airbnb is extremely important. It's not just like a store's display case to get people in; it's the store. On your advertising page, the guest decides whether or not to book your home or room. For example, if you type 'London' in the search function of Airbnb, you will find hundreds of advertisements. How do you ensure that potential guests click on your Airbnb advertisement and how do you ensure that they book with you?

A title is really meant for the reader to withdraw from your text the key information. There are many techniques to make titles as attractive as possible. At Airbnb, a lot of interesting information often works well, but the frequently used techniques in marketing also work well. Of course, it is best to use both. In blogs or articles, you often read titles such as *'5 ways to save money'* or *'the secret of a slim belly.'* These are typical marketing titles and work super well. Here you focus on something that the reader does not know but would like to know.

Your advertisement title on Airbnb is extremely important. An ad title is not defined in a hurry: it is built. To differentiate yourself from your competition and succeed in attracting the reader's attention, put yourself in his place and ask yourself what information would be hard-hitting to trigger a click. Bet on what is specific to you! The title of your ad is of utmost importance. Indeed, it is your title, with your cover photo, that will draw the attention of internet users to your ad and encourage them to click on your offer to find out the details. It should, therefore, not be left to chance.

Just as the title of a book or the name of a product directly influences its success, a catchy title will be a big part of the success of your rental. This is critical in the vacationer's choice to view your ad. The title is intended for your future customers, not for you. It is essential to see yourself as a potential guest scrolling through your listing on Airbnb. If your accommodation is in the city center, you will be the target of foreign tourists looking for beautiful views and amazing places. If your accommodation is more in the countryside, people looking for peace will find your ad. Take a look at the other Airbnb accommodation around yours. Surely there must be a bunch. How to stand out from the rest? Formulate a proposal above the lot? You need to be doing what others are not doing. You need to be ahead of the game. Follow through the following steps and build up your listing from just another ad on Airbnb to Superhost status.

NO BULLSHITTING WORDS / UNNECESSARY ADJECTIVES

Adjectives can add power to a word, but if you don't use them appropriately, they lose their power very quickly. You should only use adjectives if it really adds something new to your sentence or if the sentence is not powerful enough without it. Because often, it doesn't usually do much else. Just look at this title: *A very nice place where you can sleep well.* At first, you may think it's a good title, but if you don't know anything about an apartment and city, what do you learn from this title? You know just as much know nothing. What one person thinks is a nice place, the other can find so uninspiring.

10 minutes in Amsterdam center with free parking and WiFi: this is another title but one with so much more information. Someone who wants to visit Amsterdam by car and maybe wants to work a little more will probably click on this advertisement. This title contains many elements that are important for many travelers and will, therefore, be clicked much more than the other generic *nice* ad title. Always go with concrete words that reinforce the idea of your ads on your reader's mind. If people need to think when they read your ads, you will lose them quickly. So make sure you use specific words or words that mean the same thing to everyone. When I ask you what a papaya looks like, you probably won't be able to see that. Maybe you are thinking of something green, I thought with seeds or something, not exactly. While when I ask what an orange looks like, you immediately see an orange round fruit, with a crown on the top and small holes in the skin.

The memory works like Velcro. Velcro straps all have hooks and if something has many loops, it will catch on. The more loops (tangible memories) attached to a word, the better it stays in the memory. And that is exactly what you want, what if there is recognition in your memory, images are added, and you see it in front of you.

SURPRISE AND SPAWN YOUR READER

The reader has a certain expectation about

something and the properties they are looking out for, if you unexpectedly distort it, it'll attract attention. So by trying to put something contradictory, twisting a truth or use a bit of humor will work some wonder. Your goal is to make people curious and show that weaknesses are not bad. Give a little bit of information, twist it around a little, but above all show that there is more to be found about a certain subject. Use terms such as' benefits' secrets', 'discover', 'reason', 'why' and 'top.' However, be careful not to overshoot this tactics, by ensuring that you manage the expectations of your guests. Have a go at some of the ads below:

- Happy with a headache
- Sustained crisis gift for tourism
- 5 reasons not to become a superhost
- The secret to Airbnb that I really can't tell
- Discover how temporary rental pays for itself in 3 days

MARKETING / INFORMATIVE ADS
The disadvantage of marketing titles is that it

takes up a lot of characters to use such a technique and guest at Airbnb want to know the most important of things about their potential lodge pretty fast. Take for example, a blog or article that focuses on the reader who did not necessarily intend to read your piece, but became hooked by your title. Your guest are really looking for a stay and are looking for the best. What do you have to say about these listing titles below? Even though they tell little about the space, they are very interesting regardless.

- Five reasons to book this apartment
- Perhaps the most beautiful place in Amsterdam
- If you have slept here, you will never want to go anywhere else

There is a good chance that such a title works very well and attracts many visitors. You should actually test the titles for a while to see what works best for your ad. An even better approach is to combine a marketing title with an informative title. This way, you are providing them with just about enough important information, and teasing them to want more.

- So rural, the forester will be jealous
- In the heart of Amsterdam and five tips for free parking
- So much tranquility and yet in the center of Amsterdam

CLEAR ADS TEXTS

Clearly describe the benefits of your home. Explain what is so good, what benefits it has for the guest, and what the area has to offer. Be as complete as possible. The guests do not know things that are obvious to you. Try to put yourself in the position of your guests and think about what you would like at a holiday residence. The smallest things can provide added value. Is it quiet at night, is there a hairdryer, does the kitchen have a microwave, are they allowed to use bicycles? But also things like nice bars or breakfast places, an unobstructed view or a park nearby are valuable additions.

Sell your property as well as possible. Make sure you highlight as many interesting features as possible. If you live close to ta beautiful park, tell them what is nice about the park, if you live next to the Museum, let them what is interesting about the museums. You never can tell; that can be the thing that will draw them in and make them book your property. Many tourists are aware of certain monuments in their destination and if your advertisement states it is maybe a 5-minute walk from your place, that is a good catch. Many tourists only know a few things about a city, even about Amsterdam. So let your guests know why your city is so great.

Think of the title as the signpost that catches your guest at a distance. It has to be irresistible. You must aim to grab their attention the moment they set eye on your ad. And you cannot do all of that wit crappy text. Bold, clear, and distinct ads text is what you go for every single time. The title is extremely important for an Airbnb advertisement. It helps the title, and I cannot emphasize enough the importance of your ad title. The title is actually the display of your Airbnb store. Take the time to do that, because if your title is not right, people will not click on it and your text that you have tossed so hard on will not even be read. The title makes you stand out among those hundreds of advertisements. If many people view your ad, you not only have a better chance of booking, it is also good for your score in the Airbnb search engine. Therefore, write an irresistible title for Airbnb visitors.

WRITE EXPRESSIVELY AND CONCRETELY

Take the reader into your story. Let him really feel like he is already in your apartment and he not only reads what you write, but sees it before him. You do that by writing expressively and concretely. For example, if you write that there is a park next to your home, that is a fact and it doesn't do much to you. But if you take the reader into the park, your story comes to life: 'You wake up, walk to the window and open the curtains. The sun's rays shine through the window so hard that your eye has to get used to it. You can see the park from the room. What could be nicer than having breakfast at a beautiful scenic park? You look for a nice spot by the water, the birds whistle on it and on a rug you put the freshly baked rolls, fresh fruit, and orange juice. Your partner takes your hand and says: "Shall we go to the museum today?" This will be a beautiful day. "

In the example above you notice that you are included in the story. Don't be afraid to write so narratively. You will notice that people like to read and will switch sooner. In this piece, it is of course, very expressively written and you tell it extensively, but not very much. What you know from this is that you overlook the park and it feels as if there is an oven. Therefore try to find a good balance between giving information and writing.

Now you ask yourself, how do you write expressively? The answer is not farfetched. With visual writing, you ensure that the reader sees the story that's in front of you and not only reads it from a computer screen. With visual writing, you focus on what happens, not the action itself: 'The wheels clatter over the rails. The trees shoot past me and I see the station approach. Just when I think he continues, I hear the brakes beeping. A group of people is waiting on the platform. The driver stops so that the door opens exactly for the passengers. "I did not tell you that I am on the train, but you know it and you see yourself on the train that arrives at a station. Think carefully about what exactly happens, pay close attention to the details and use visual words.

SPECIAL FEATURES

Many travelers use Airbnb because they are looking for a home or apartment with more character and authenticity than a standard hotel room in a tourist area. Use the description of your accommodation to indicate what makes this lodge so special. This can be, for example, the good location of the property, but also the distinct architecture or the interesting historical background of the property. Every accommodation has its own advantages. How do you do this? By making use of a catchy title to quickly draw your reader to take notice of that special feature. If a tree falls in the woods, and there is no one present to see or hear it, did it make a sound? Of course not. So in the same manner, the special features that your house has got are useless if no one is seeing that it has it in the first place.

When you have determined what makes your space unique, it is important to process this information in the title of your AirBnB page. There will be numerous providers who advertise with generic keywords such as' spacious', light 'and' centrally located '. You will not stand out with this. Instead, choose a title that appeals to the imagination and explains why your AirBnB not only offers guests a stay but a complete experience. It will help you to have a Unique Selling Point (USP). A unique selling point is more like your strong suit. Something that makes your property stands out. One of the best ways to emerge from the crowd is to define your market position. A clear positioning helps your customer target to understand what you offer different than competitors. You have to think of a strong identity. Watch Airbnb that has clearly defined its positioning: a platform for travelers who want to live a personalized travel experience. At the same instance, it has created a unique opportunity for those people who want to earn extra money by earning a room. The best way to define your position is to develop your own unique selling point USP. The USP describes the unique benefits and advantages that your place offers. It must be clear, concise and easy to understand.

YOUR TITLE MUST MATCH YOUR POTENTIAL CUSTOMERS

By the use of search filters, your travelers also have expectations regarding the service they hope to have thanks to Airbnb. So, by targeting a city, a district of Paris, a number of beds and rooms, a price range, your future travelers have already stated a precise idea of what they are looking for. Because of the brevity of writing the title, everything in your Airbnb ad must best meet the criteria that define your traveler base. From your host point of view, by renting your property on Airbnb, you most certainly have an idea of the type of travelers you would like to have at home. Give them what they expect.

Don't settle for a descriptive title, it will get you nowhere. As we saw in the paragraph above, your future guest has already expressed the type of accommodation he is looking for. No need to weigh down your title by adding the characteristics of your accommodation. As an example, if you have a property that is perfect for families because of its size and its facilities, it is useless to specify it in the title: in addition to the criterion of the number of travelers already defined which filters the accommodation having Adequate reception capacity, the Families collection, a filter designed by Airbnb if you meet specific criteria, will highlight your advertisement in this customer segment. Also, the space you have to write the title of your ad is precious: emphasize what makes your accommodation unique.

DO NOT INCLUDE UNNECESSARY LOCATION INFORMATION

We saw it in the first paragraph of this part

devoted to the writing of the title: your future guest has already expressed a certain number of characteristics that he or she is looking for, including the location of the desired accommodation. He or she has a relatively precise idea of where your accommodation is located; appending the city name at the end of the title brings little value to your travelers.

On the other hand, indicating the presence of a tourist major place or a beach in the surroundings or the name of a popular district are entirely relevant aspects and likely to cause travelers to want to click on your ad rather than on competing advertisements having more or less the same characteristics (type of accommodation, number of beds, price, location).

CHANGE YOUR TITLE REGULARLY

Travelers' desires vary according to the seasons. For example, a rental in Nice will be very beneficial to highlight the joys of the

Mediterranean in summer and those of the mountains of the hinterland. And get to know your typical travelers, so as to know how to change things up a bit whenever there is the need for it. Before writing the body of your ad, keep in mind that you have identified one or more types of travelers desired and that, conversely, the characteristics of your accommodation will attract a specific type of guests. This involves the use of vocabulary, keywords that can speak to your target audience.

ADOPT A TONE TO YOUR IMAGE

As the angle of a photo is important, the perception of your ad depends largely on the tone you adopt. Even if this plays out in a more or less perceptible way, your Airbnb travelers will immediately have an image of their hosts. The way you write reflects your personality. Airbnb is a platform connecting individuals. It is better to adopt a relatively informal tone. As a tip, imagining how it would be yours if you were to describe your accommodation to a friend is a good way to find the right tone. Focus on what's unique about your home. And really about what is unique. In the Airbnb ad, it is important to press on what differentiates your accommodation from your competitors.

BE CONCISE AND TO THE POINT

Writing your Airbnb ad is also a concise exercise. This involves gathering and organizing the information you deem useful and relevant through short, clear sentences or even bullet points.

To fully appreciate the importance of this point, think about the time you spend browsing an Airbnb ad when you find yourself on the traveler side looking for the best possible accommodation: in general, travelers quickly review the description of the property. 'ad by targeting information they deem relevant. The type of information sought varies according to the prism of each traveler; that is why clarity and conciseness are essential.

However, conciseness does not imply too much brevity, even if the time spent reading the description of an advertisement is on average relatively low. Writing too short would be perceived as a lack of involvement on your part and would give the impression that you had partly botched your advertisement.

COMPLETE THE OTHER SECTIONS IN DETAIL

The rest of the other sections are optional but not less important. According to Airbnb, only 30% of hosts fill them out. Therefore this turns out to be an advantage to get noticed. The title of your Airbnb ad is, along with the photo, one of the two essential parameters of your ad. I exclude here the price and the location, which are filtered beforehand by the visitor before the ads appear in the search results. Most hosts do not pay much attention to the title of their advertisement. They prefer to optimize their pricing. This is understandable, it is an important selection criterion. But between two equivalent prices, which ad will they click on first?

CHAPTER SIX

WHAT IS THE BEST PRICING STRATEGY: MARKET RESEARCH AND HOW TO FIND BEST ROI AIRBNB PROPERTIES IN YOUR AREA

Being an Airbnb host can be really challenging and rewarding at the same time. And if you are doing it carefully, you can also earn some decent money. But you can't make the most of your ad without the right pricing strategy. So what is the pricing strategy you should use? Well, the strategies are simple, but implementation takes some work.

After the periods of doubt and the many preparations, you have finally decided to start your listing on Airbnb to rent to tourists and earn some money but, after the initial enthusiasm, you realized that reservations are scarce. At this point you asked yourself what the reasons may be and you have doubted that perhaps you are applying the wrong rate. So, how do you fix it? If you are asking yourself this kind of doubts today is your lucky day. I will walk you through the proven methods that have worked for me over the years on how to set the right price on Airbnb, and in general on all real estate brokerage portals. In this chapter, I am going to help you understand how to set the right rate to maximize your profit. Take some time for yourself and continue reading: in a few minutes you will finally be able to understand how to choose the optimal rate and increase bookings!

THE IMPORTANCE OF THE RIGHT PRICE: CLIMB THE RANKING AND SELL

The first thing to clarify is how important the price is not only for selling, but also for positioning on the search engines of the portals. A rate does not necessarily have to be the lowest of all, but must be competitive in relation to similar structures that offer comparable services (accessories, location, finishes, parking, etc.). We happened to have to deal with owners who complained about not receiving reservations, despite applying a very low price. It can happen, especially if the structure lacks some essential services or management errors have been made.

Choosing the right price is essential: if it is too high it drives reservations away, if it is too low it burns potential earnings. In addition, the portals take this into account in their ranking , that is, the order chosen in showing the structures to the interested parties: if the accommodation has an inconvenient quality-price ratio, it will end up at the bottom! On the other hand, the goal of the portals is to sell, and to do so they must encourage the most promising structures!

HOW TO GET STARTED

If you are a beginner, the easiest way to find the right price is to watch your competition, or the ads with which you will be competing on Airbnb. Once I would have told you to do this research on your own, now I tell you instead of using a tool like **AirDNA** - it saves you hours and allows you to have an immediate view of your market and competition.

Start By Doing Market Research

I call it the act of studying your competition. Start with a property similar to yours in the same area: something with the same number of beds, quality, services, etc. You find out how much do they ask on weekdays and weekends? Study the calendar for the whole year by searching in the middle of the month for each month. It will take some time, but it will not only give you a sense of the prices in the market but also if there is a high and low season throughout the year. Use this as a starting point for prices.

Check Hotels in Your Area

Especially if you can't find any comparable property on Airbnb, just look at how much single room hotels cost on average. At this point, set up your ad on Airbnb at a cost of at least 25-30% lower. For larger properties, the price increases by 35% for each additional room. Now decide on which of the following pricing strategies you want to base your ad on. In the short-term rental market, you are not alone; indeed portals such as Airbnb and Booking.com see a constant growth of partners every year. This means that in order to set the right price and emerge it is essential to know your competitors, study their moves, and act accordingly, always being aware of the differences.

Who your Competitor is and How to Spot them

A competitor is that structure similar to yours in characteristics and located in a reasonably close area. This means that if there are 100 other hosts in your country, they are not necessarily all your competitors, but you must be able to identify only those who offer a service comparable to yours in a limited radius. So, if you manage a budget holiday home, for example, in the center of Milan, you will not have to compare yourself to an economic one in the suburbs, as you will not be able to compare yourself to luxury across the street.

Once the competitors have been identified, the next move is to do better than them. How? Keeping a slightly lower price is an option, and it is also the one most rewarded by the portals ... but it is not the only one. For example, you can try to keep a similar or slightly higher rate while increasing the services and the perceived quality. It is a question of giving the person concerned the impression of making a real deal by booking a well-equipped accommodation at the right price. There are various techniques for implementing this second option; the right strategy depends on the type of accommodation you are proposed to manage. For example, improving the appearance of the apartment through a Home Staging operation can have a significant impact on booking requests and therefore, on earnings. Even enriching the accommodation with the right accessories can make a big difference, provided they have a concrete value for the tourist.

THE IMPORTANCE OF MARKETING STRATEGIES FOR AIRBNB

If marketing strategies are the necessary precondition for guaranteeing the success of any commercial activity, they are even more indispensable in the management of Airbnb, an organization based exclusively on interpersonal communication. Being on the platform with a marketing strategy that involves all the usable media represents a very important requirement to conquer large slices of users.

An articulated and correctly structured strategy on the web, therefore, guarantees unquestionable advantages in the management of structures on Airbnb, so word of mouth and positive references available online represent only the first prerequisites that are indispensable but not sufficient to really a breakthrough. Thanks to the fact that this organization addresses a wide range of customers, including individuals belonging to any income group, from the super-rich to those who are struggling at the end of the month, its impact on tourism is highly significant given that it encourages travel also subjects who otherwise would have renounced this opportunity.

The main strength of Airbnb is to directly involve people who intend to interface with each other, stimulating their participation in the community. The most used technique is that of content-marketing, capable of establishing a reliable and lasting relationship with customers through the sharing of multimedia content on the platform by those who tell their travel experience, also through videos and photos, and make publish their considerations and judgments on rented homes and hosts. A practice that, if well exploited, helps to spread (and advertise) the structures on the portal, guaranteeing the huge host revenues and important positions on the Airbnb pages. Being well positioned on the portal, and having always positive reviews, is a fundamental step to make this activity a profitable and successful commitment.

Same Quality / Lower Price

Close the gap between your property and your similar competitors. Same services, a better price equals better value. This pricing strategy is great for mid-level or cheaper ads. However, this type of strategy can only get you so far. It is best for when you are starting out and want to get in the reviews to boost your profile.

Better Quality / Same Price

You own all the services of the competition with better quality but at the same price. This strategy is ideal for more luxurious ads that have a clear advantage over the competition. After all, when a potential guest is comparing your ad to other ads, your goal is for that guest to perceive more value in your ad. This is a great strategy to have the upper hand over your close competitor. Guest will start seeing you as the better deal and will always look to book you solid.

Offer Something Different

Start by looking for what's missing in the area, and how you can begin to offer that. Smaller areas often have missing categories and services. Try to position your property in the area by providing something missing. Then wait some time to see if this leads to the increase in requests or reservations. If not, find something else to try for your ad. Example: include a free voucher for the nearest garage or free tickets for public transport. Guests will surely appreciate it.

Automated Pricing

If you really want to boost your return on investment (ROI) with an effective pricing strategy, then you will have to automate it. Price automation is about having a system that automatically updates prices based on changes in local demand that it collects using a huge amount of data analysis. Automated pricing has helped some hosts earn up to 40% more by saving potentially "lost" bookings. Just as prices can sometimes be up to 50% higher than the prices recommended by Airbnb Smart Pricing.

Positioning Strategies: Understand How to Present Yourself

Lowering the price isn't always the right choice; on the contrary, sometimes it's the wrong one ... it depends. Let's go in order. One of the first things we need to do in our job of managing short-term apartments is to understand in which segment the property placed at our disposal by the owner falls. In principle, the main categories are:

- **Low Budget**: These are simple apartments with essential furnishings, often located in decentralized areas. These are usually accommodations for which the owner does not intend to invest large sums in modernization and therefore are intended to compete on the price. It is not necessarily a negative factor, as long as the pricing policy is kept under strict control in order to always be competitive with competitors and not lose out.

- **Medium**: We are talking about finished properties with many services, usually in a favorable position. This is a particularly delicate category since, being very numerous, if good communication and a differentiation policy with respect to the competition are not implemented, there is a risk of a painful price war. Try to always understand what the identity of the property on which to focus can be, enhancing it and distinguishing it from competitors.

- **Luxury**: This grouping includes villas and apartments with exclusive furnishings equipped with every comfort. They are usually located in central areas and perfectly served, and apply high prices. If the character of the accommodation is correctly communicated, the competition is low, and the quality of the guests high, usually being families or businessmen. In these cases, care must be taken to maintain a high level of service: the guest expects the maximum and will not easily forgive any carelessness.

Identifying the right strategy is fundamental, and it is an analysis that must be done with the utmost coherence and impartiality: the wrong category or refraining from choosing it will inevitably involve significant losses of money.

HOW TO BE SUCCESSFUL WITH AIRBNB STARTING FROM THE HOST FIGURE

The figure of the host represents the foundation for a correct management of an apartment on Airbnb because, from his behavior, his honesty and reliability, the turnover connected to the housing structure in his possession, and made available will depend. If the owner is the one who earns the greater part of the global income deriving from the lease, Airbnb derives its profit from the commissions applied on the rents, corresponding to a figure between 6% and 12% of what the guest paid. Given that the housing solutions available on the platform are extremely diverse: they range from individual rooms in apartments used by the owner to entire homes (often second homes), the resulting turnover is highly variable depending on the situation.

To incentivize the business deriving from this type of activity, Airbnb has established the figure of the "Superhost", consisting of a type of premium account recognized to landlords with a good number of five-star reviews, which are characterized by a low percentage of cancellations, and that respond quickly to requests. The Superhost status has numerous advantages, including that of having high visibility and being able to take advantage of some additional services offered by Airbnb such as, for example, the presence of a professional photographer to advertise their proposals better. According to the opinion of some super hosts, people who are particularly competent in this sector, there are some requirements whose value proves to be fundamental to guarantee the success of their accommodation.

AIRBNB PLUS

In 2018 Airbnb launched, through an update, the figure of the "Superhost," which concerns the owners who have distinguished themselves more in the management of the temporary leases of their apartments.

To be part of Airbnb Plus, listings must have some specific requirements:

- availability of a private bathroom;
- housing solution located in a specific city (there is a specific list);
- average rating obtained not less than 4.8 stars;

- lack of cancellations in the previous twelve months.

It is necessary to follow a series of stages, to be part of Airbnb Plus, including numerous mandatory steps:

- publish the advertisement exclusively with Airbnb Plus, by disconnecting from any other booking website;
- submit your housing solution to a home visit by local Airbnb partners, who must personally verify the presence of the existing requirements;
- pay a fee related to the Airbnb Plus program, which covers the necessary expenses;
- create a photoshoot with Airbnb partners;
- adapt to the report on the apartment, which is drawn up at the end of the visit and which contributes to providing suggestions and advice to improve housing conditions;
- post the ad on Airbnb Plus.

Requirements for Inclusion in Airbnb Plus

There are four pre-requisites necessary to be registered with Airbnb Plus:

- **Comfort**: Depending on the guest's ratings, the Superhost will have to make their stay as comfortable as possible to encourage the number of positive ratings. To obtain favorable reviews, it is recommended that check-in is quick and easy, that the bedrooms have comfortable beds with modern and clean mattresses and at least two pillows for each guest. Bathrooms must be hygienically adequate, preferably with a set of towels and bathrobe provided. Finally, privacy must be guaranteed through the use of curtains, shutters, or shutters that can isolate the rooms from the external environment.
- **Design**: Hosts who want to place their apartment in the Airbnb Plus category must pay particular attention to the style and furnishings of their home, which must be modern, tidy, personalized and stylish but, at the same time, functional and harmonious.

- **Maintenance**: The apartments that are part of the Airbnb Plus program must undergo regular maintenance, both as regards the external spaces (gardens or courtyards), and for the internal ones, with furnishings in good condition and clean and intact wall structures. An aspect of considerable importance is that relating to air conditioning which must guarantee comfortable living conditions, finally, water availability must be unlimited. Enrollment in the Airbnb Plus program costs around 120 euros, which are considered as a sort of spending fund for all the services offered.
- **Equipment**: The services offered by the apartments belonging to the Airbnb Plus category necessarily include fully functional and fast Wi-Fi, a television with entertainment options such as Netflix and/or Sky, security systems equipped with anti-smoke detectors or dangerous fumes, and all essential accessories for cooking and personal hygiene.

The numerous advantages of this program include:

- greater confidence from the guests, also deriving from the greater visibility of the advertisement;
- a look specially designed to make your ad stand out;
- high photographic quality;
- a virtual tour of the entire property.

CHAPTER SEVEN

HOW TO HANDLE YOUR GUESTS DURING THEIR STAY AND AFTER THEY LEAVE

One of the best ways to reach Superhost status real quick on Airbnb is to rack up great reviews. You can't do this by only listing your property on the platform; you have to give them a good experience. This has a lot to do with the way you handle their stay with you. Thoughtful thinking and little act of kindness here and there like picking them up from the airport, suggesting a cool spot for them to have a wonderful time out and so on. All of these add to the kind of overall experience that they have staying in your place. I will quickly go over different manners of ways that you can use to show a kind gesture towards your guests and to always have the perfect interaction with your guests at all times.

HOW CAN I WELCOME MY GUEST?

Welcoming your guests can be done in many ways. In the form of picking them up, or warm reception at your lodge, over the phone greeting, and a whole lot of creative ways. I'll like to tell you a story about one of the encounters I had with a host. I'll tell you how the most adorable Airbnb hosts from Naples, Carlo and Michela welcomed me. Meanwhile, the friendliness began already during the exchange of messages before arrival. I wanted a flexible check-in , and it wasn't a problem for them. Upon arrival, they opened the door to us smiling two young boys and on the bed, we found the following:

Nothing was missing, from towels to welcome chocolate. A complete bathroom kit (categorically pink for me and blue for my travel companion). A note was written in their own hand, which I still keep. The map of Naples and some prices of local attractions. And finally, they immediately invited us to a concert for the same evening, leaving us free to refuse. But the thing that struck me most is the wall on which guests can leave messages and drawings. In short, an Airbnb experience with counter bows. I think it is natural for them to be so damn perfect, but you don't have to be outdone!

One thing you can add is fun signs that help the guest feel at home. Where are the keys? What is its shelf in the cupboard? How do you turn on the heating? What about the Wi-Fi password? These are things that you will show them in person, but which certainly in the tiredness of the arrival could be forgotten.

WHAT ARE THE SAFETY RULES?

It is like health, as long as there is no one thinks about it. Instead, in terms of security, it is better to prevent than to cure, and Airbnb knows it well. Do you think you can buy on their website a smoke detector and carbon monoxide, which arrives directly at home - you will be deducted the price from the next bookings. Another thing that Airbnb offers you is a security card with emergency telephone numbers, where there are fire hazard alarms and fire extinguishers and any evacuation plan.

BE A GOOD HOST

Having someone stay in your house can have countless benefits. I like the intimate air and the feeling of living almost in a parallel dimension, which you still feel yours. However, it is important to ensure that they are aware that it is not really like staying in a hotel.

In short, make them feel at home. Have respect for the things for their privacy; do not leave dirt around or try to oversee things too much. If anything, communicate in an open and sociable way. If there is something wrong, tell your guests immediately without waiting for it to get worse or ruin their holiday. For the house rules, I recommend that you let them know of it as soon as possible; the earlier, the better, with the house rules carefully located on the tab of each apartment. If they travel with pets, make sure they are welcome. Some houses, on the other hand, are not suitable for children (perhaps because they have precious furnishings) or the hosts place limitations that do not go well with their travel and lifestyle.

CAPTURE ATTENTION FROM THE

VERY FIRST SEARCH

The search for a trip usually starts 80 days even before their departure. This is the stage where travelers still don't have clear ideas on where to go and spend many hours on the internet and social networks looking for inspiration on their next holidays. It is at this moment that you package engaging content that immediately catches the user's attention. It focuses on high-quality images, emotional videos, blog articles that tell the experiences to do at the destination, the scheduled events, and the attractions to visit. In this way, you will create a direct link between the structure you manage and the location where it is located. Why never forget: travelers look first for the destination, then for the accommodation to book.

While at it, don't forget to make the offer interesting and catchy. The sooner you get the booking, the more the costs of your online and offline promotional campaigns will decrease. Use the data collected by Google Analytics and other analysis platforms to find the best time of the month or year to send your offers by email and promote them online on Google or Facebook. Make personalized offers based on your previous experience and insights.

PERSONALIZE TO RETAIN

Strategic and careful planning after getting the booking helps you to win the customer's trust. If you are able to retain the customer right away, cancellations of reservations will decrease. We refer above all to reservations that require free cancellation, and another option is the instant booking. Furthermore, if at this stage you establish a strong relationship with the customer, becoming in his eyes a reliable host and an authentic connoisseur of the destination, it is very likely that at the end of the stay, the guest will become a return customer.

To have loyal customers, focus on personalizing your stay. Often the customer buys the most useful services as soon as he books. Study the customer and the relative booking to offer them valuable services that really help them plan their holiday better. For example, do not suggest renting a scooter to a couple with an infant. Rather, offer him the shuttle from the airport.

In fact, as soon as you receive the booking, direct or from an OTA, you can directly customize the offer by sending push notifications to them. In this way, you'll prove yourself a reliable but not intrusive host. All this even before his arrival at the facility!

UPSELL JUST BEFORE ARRIVAL

Usually, during the travel, the traveler purchases essential services as soon as he books. While postponing the booking of the activities to do at your destination a few hours before departure or immediately after arrival. Customized travel experiences are an exception and a key component of giving your guest a fun-filled experience. There are diverse activities you can take your guest to do that will not only allow you to earn more but also give them a more wonderful traveling experience.

CUSTOMER RELATION BEYOND CHECKOUT

Just as the good customer service starts from

the travel research phase. So it doesn't end with checkout. If you have done exceptionally well up to that point, you will have worked well to improve the guest experience, at the end of their stay, you will have an additional loyal customer. And above all, you will have earned a positive review.

Immediately at the end of your stay, you must urge the customer to leave an online review. You can as well do it very discreetly. Over the following weeks, based on the valuable information that you have certainly collected about the customer, you will have to send him personalized offers to involve him: exciting new experiences, irresistible proposals, events scheduled at the destination.

CHAPTER EIGHT

HOW TO BECOME AIRBNB SUPERHOST

You have read up to this point and have discovered a lot of tricks and tips to get your Airbnb business started and make it a success. Now your hosting business on Airbnb is live and now you wonder how to get better results? Have you noticed the famous badge around, and now you wonder what the Airbnb Superhost is and how it works? You wonder how to become Superhost, and especially what benefits? Quiet, these are legitimate questions that many ask themselves, and in this chapter, I will try to clarify this often underestimated and poorly understood figure.

In addition to the information made available by Airbnb on the subject, I have come up with this definitive guide with suggestions taken from reputable hosts in the business. This is committed to helping other hosts maximize the rent of their apartment by providing them with ideas that will be of great help. So are you ready? You have to relax, take a few minutes and read each paragraph carefully. At the end of the reading, you will know the meaning of Superhost in addition to the tricks that could simplify your life in an attempt to grab the famous badge! Very well, let's get started!

WHO IS A SUPERHOST?

Let's start by clarifying what the Airbnb Superhost is. The "Superhost" is a simple host which, however, has distinguished itself among others for having achieved high-quality standards through its exceptional service to guests, or has been able to offer its guests high-level stay experiences. The super hosts are therefore owners or managers of highly experienced apartments, which represent a point of reference for both the other hosts and the guests: the latter will have the certainty (or almost) of having to deal with a severe and reliable owner, and the service offered rhodium and commonly appreciated.

A host who achieves this status is awarded by Airbnb with a special badge in the shape of a medal, which will be placed in view next to his profile picture. We specify that the status of Superhost is a recognition that remains tied to the manager of the accommodation, not to the apartment. This means that a person could manage five apartments and appear on each of them with this badge, making each accommodation benefit from it. However, the reverse is also true, which means that the Superhost "draws strength" from the apartments he manages: the reviews given by the guests of all his accommodations will determine his status, and therefore decree the beginning or end of this recognition.

How to become Superhost? Airbnb requirements and considerations

Four times a year (once every 3 months), Airbnb makes a mapping of all its hosts with the aim of verifying which of them, in the last 12 months, has managed to meet the requirements of the Superhost and who instead can no longer join it because of a drop in performance. Let's clarify the concept of the previous 12 months with an example. At the moment, Airbnb checks the requirements on

January 1st, April 1st, July 1st and October 1st of each year, referring to the period of one year prior to the valuation date. So if for example, in the period April 1, 2018 - April 1, 2019, you were not suitable, but between April 2019 and July 2019 you managed to obtain a series of excellent results, it could be that at the next check-in July, which refers to the period July 2018 - July 2019 you are in a position to win the Superhost badge.

It goes without saying that, as time passes, results older than one year completely lose its value. This may be good or bad, but it certainly gives those who have had the misfortune of getting a series of bad reviews to "get rid of" them for the purpose of this recognition. What is the requirement for becoming a Superhost is one of the most common questions asked by hosts. The requirements, which have recently been updated, are basically the following:

- At least **50% of guests must leave a review**: It's not one of the biggest hurdles since most guests usually leave a review, but that's not said. Based on our experience, we have noticed that a simple trick to increase the percentage of reviews is to talk about it with the guest at the time of check out, asking if it is the stay went well and communicating that his opinion would be highly appreciated. Generally, the guest is happy to know that his opinion is welcome, and will help you by leaving a comment

- Have **more than 10 active stays**: This point aims to ensure guests are dealing with owners who have considerable experience behind them. Attention, we are not talking about reviews, but about **stays**. This means that if you host nine groups and each of them leaves a review, this will still not be enough to meet the required standards. An equally valid alternative is to have at least 100 nights in the last year from a minimum of 3 different guests. This option is designed not to penalize those who offered long-term stays.

- **No cancellation**: Leaving for a holiday with suitcases in hand, having your reservation canceled can be traumatizing, and the search for new accommodation at the last moment can create enormous inconvenience. For this reason, Airbnb grants the renowned badge only to those who have not canceled any reservations in the last year, proving to be organized and reliable hosts.

- **Response rate of** at least **90% within 24 hours**: In other words, 90% of the request messages must find a response from the host within a maximum of one day. This is a parameter of timeliness which, is also fundamental for maximizing the conversion of your ad. You will need a dedicated team that takes care of responding promptly to requests; this is because even a delay of a few minutes can give the guest the opportunity to find another solution. The same applies during your stay: when you are traveling and some needs arise, the guest wants to be sure that he is dealing with an interlocutor present, who responds closely and not after three days!

- **Ensure to have an average review rating of at least 4.8 out of 5:** This is perhaps the most difficult parameter to achieve, as an average of 4.8 stars out of a maximum of 5 is really complicated to achieve: just a 3-star rating is enough to be forced to replicate with nine 5-star reviews, without talking about what would happen with a worse grade. In short, you need to pay close attention to the needs of the guest, and it may not be enough: for example, in our experience as managers of short-term rental apartments, we have read amazing reviews associated with a 4-star rating. This is because each of us gives its own meaning to this measurement, and maybe for someone four is an excellent judgment, but it is not for the host. Also, in this case, it may be important to communicate to the guest the meaning and weight of his judgments.

Advantages, Rewards, and Benefits: Because It Is Better To Be an Airbnb Superhost

You have to ask yourself at this point, with all the effort that needs to be done to win the coveted recognition, what are the advantages of being an Airbnb Superhost. Let's start by debunking a myth: being Superhost, by Airbnb's own admission, does not entitle you to particular advantages as regards the ranking of your accommodations. In other words, being a Superhost will not make the search results rankings on your ad, far from it: you will continue to compete with other owners according to normal market dynamics.

The real advantages of being a Superhost are others: let us discover them one by one.

- **High index of reliability and professionalism**: Put yourself in the shoes of Mario, a guest who is looking for accommodation for his vacation. Mario has already identified the area in which to stay but is undecided between a couples of solutions. One of these costs slightly more but is managed by a Superhost. Although Mario intends to book cheap accommodation, his priority is not to have any surprises during his stay, so he will be more likely to book the Superhost's accommodation as this status reassures him and puts him at ease.

- **Greater earnings**: Airbnb says that those who are awarded the famous badge can earn up to 22% more. It is not so clear whether this is the result of the greater bookings that can be received or the higher price that can be applied based on this status. Probably a combination of the two.
- **Exclusive prizes**: If you manage to keep your badge for a year, you will be given a $ 100 voucher that can be spent on the site for your travels. This award will be repeated for every year!
- **Superhost filter**: In the search menu, Airbnb gives the possibility to apply a series of filters, including that of Superhost: by checking it, only those owners who fall into this category will be shown, cutting out all the others. It

goes without saying that if a guest applies this filter, your line of competitors will be significantly reduced, and it will, therefore, be much easier for the interested party to choose you.

- **+ 20% bonus for inviting new hosts**: Airbnb rewards those who convince other hosts to sign up to the portal with an amount of money that can be spent on their site. If you are a Superhost, this benefit will be increased by 20%.
- **Advertising emails**: From time to time, Airbnb sends guests lists of accommodation of possible interest, inviting them to visit the relevant pages to find out more. If you are a holder of the renowned badge, you will be included in these lists, and you'll, therefore, have a far better chance of winning reservations.

HOW TO STAY SUPERHOST: PROVEN METHOD

We have seen that being a Superhost entitles you too many interesting advantages. We have also seen, however, that every three months the platform checks whether the requirements for continuing to be part of this category remain, and if this is not the case, the aforementioned status is lost. So how do you keep the Superhost badge for as long as possible? We would like to give you some advice from our experience as apartment managers.

- **Clear and concise house rules**: There is a section of the ad description where you are called to write the house rules. We recommend to insert any limit or constraint to which the guests will be subjected, for example, silence times, the maximum ambient temperature in winter, tourist taxes or taxes not specified elsewhere etc., this to avoid unpleasant last-minute surprises for the guest.
- **Maximum availability and timeliness**: Tell the guest that you are at his disposal, ask him how the trip went,

and during his stay, offer him advice on where to eat and what places to visit, answer all his questions promptly. The personal relationship has enormous value on Airbnb.

- **Create expectations that you can meet:** It may happen that you are tempted to write descriptions to the limit of truth with the intent to grab some more reservations. It is not wrong to "bows" your own accommodation, but if the customer who has booked does not find what he was expecting, then he will be disappointed. We suggest a more cautious approach, that is, on the one hand, to entice the guest to book, but on the other to keep a few tricks up their sleeve for when they arrive. For example, it'd be an honest idea to give him a welcome basket with water, chocolates, and maybe a bottle of wine. You will see that he will appreciate it and take it into account in the evaluation!
- **No improvisation, be professional**: Even if managing an apartment is not your main job, you

have to do it as if it were. Enter the mind of a hotelier: you must be ready if a pipe breaks on Sunday or if the boiler stops working at dinner time. The fact that it is not a hotel does not exempt you from offering professional service.

Printed in Great Britain
by Amazon